The Lost Den

by Catherine Baker

illustrated by Marina Perez Luque

OXFORD
UNIVERSITY PRESS

Daisy was bursting with excitement. Her family was going camping with Granny! Granny made everything fun.

At the campsite, Mum and Dad put up the tents. Daisy and Granny went exploring.

The campsite was on a farm.

“Look, donkeys!” called Daisy.

Granny looked around.

“I visited this farm as a girl!” she said.

"Once, I made a den," said Granny.
"It was in a hollow tree."

“Let’s look for your den,” said Daisy.

“I expect it’s disappeared,” said Granny sadly.

That evening, Mum gathered wood for the fire.
Dad made beans on toast for tea.

Soon, it was bedtime. Daisy made a plan about Granny's den.

Daisy would look for the den tomorrow.
She was sure Granny would be pleased.

The next day was sunny.
Let me show you the places I went, Daisy.

Daisy and Granny saw cows being milked.
They saw hens laying eggs.

They had fresh eggs for lunch!

Then Daisy and Mum went to the woods.

"Let's play hide-and-seek!" said Daisy.
"You hide, I'll count," said Mum.

Daisy looked for a place to hide. Suddenly, she saw one!

It was a hollow tree. Daisy crawled into the wide hole.

Mum was still counting. Daisy waited.
The hole made a good den.

Daisy saw a little gap. She put her hand in to see.

She pulled out a carved wooden donkey.
The name 'Sue Dean' was on it.

"That's Granny!" gasped Daisy.

Mum was astonished to see the donkey.
This must be Granny's den!

Daisy sprinted back to their tents.

"Granny! Come and see!" Daisy shouted.

Granny entered the snug den. She took her donkey, and gave Daisy a hug.

"I lost my den and my donkey. Now you have found them," Granny said. "Thank you, Daisy."

Look Back

Encourage students to use the pictures to retell the story.